Actually Useful Accounting

I0471086

by Phil Cohen

Contents

Introduction

I've been running consulting and training businesses in Sydney, Australia for 30 years. This book is designed for people who run - or are going to run - a business. There is nothing in here that you don't need, and a lot of stuff that you do need that you won't find anywhere else.

Phil Cohen, Sydney, 2013

The accounting equation

No matter how much a robot might look like a person, it doesn't have the same rights as a person: in particular, it can't own property.

What has this to do with accounting?

Well, a company is sort of like a robot: legally it's considered a sort of person, but an inferior type of person because it can't really own anything.

A company's **assets** (things it has) always equal what it owes. If a company pays all of what it owes (including what it owes to its owners) then it will use up all of its assets and have nothing left.

So like a robot, a company can't own anything: everything it has it owes to someone else.

There's a special name for what the company owes its *owners*; it's called **equity**. Other kinds of debts are called **liabilities**. So for any company, what it company has = what it owes.

So *assets* are what a company has.

Equity is what it owes to its owners.

Liabilities are what it owes to people other than its owners.

Let's look at an example. You set up a company and put $10 into its bank account. The company now has assets (things it has) of $10, and its equity (the amount it owes you, its owner) is $10.

Now let's say that the company gets a bill for $1 for rent. It now has a liability (something it owes to someone *other* than its owners) of $1. It still has $10 in the bank (because it hasn't paid the bill yet so all of that original $10 is still there) so if assets ($10) = liabilities ($1) + equity, then the equity must now be $9.

Another way of saying this is that the company is now 'worth' only $9. The value of the company has reduced to $9, and that's how much the company now owes to you, its owner. So if the company was 'dissolved' paid the bill and closed down the bank account, there would be $9 left for you to pick up.

This equation (assets = liabilities + equity) is called the ***accounting equation***. Like much of accounting, it's actually pretty simple.

Question

A company has assets of $5 and liabilities of $3. What is the value of the equity in that company?

Answer

$2

Explanation

From the accounting equation: assets ($5) = liabilities ($3) + equity (must be $2). So if you formed the company by putting $5 into its bank account (company assets now $5) but it got a rent bill for $3 (liability) then if the company paid its bills and then paid everything it had back to the owner, you'd get $2.

Double entry

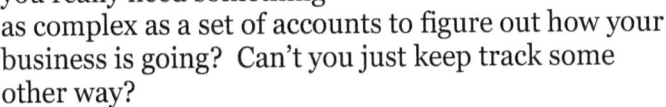

The point of accounting is
... just counting money. Do
you really need something
as complex as a set of accounts to figure out how your
business is going? Can't you just keep track some
other way?

Let's look at a simple business: a shop. At the end of
each day you'll want to know how you have done, so
you'll probably print a list of sales from the till. This
will tell you how much money you've taken in during
the day, and also (hopefully!) how much cash is in the
till. Simple enough.

And you might also want to know how much you
spent during the day, so you look at your cheque
stubs and count how much money went out of your
bank account.

To find out how much money you made on the day,
you simply subtract the spending from the sales. That
gives you your profit for the day.

Now yes, that would work perfectly well for the very
simplest of businesses, and if your business is really
that simple then you don't need accounting: just keep
a diary of money in and money out.

But there is probably no business on the planet that's
that simple.

For example, let's say that one day your best
customer leaves their wallet at home. They buy
something from your shop, and you agree to let them
pay the next day.

Does that count as a sale for the day? Yes it does. But
does the money end up in the till that day? No. So

your simple model of counting the till to work out your sales for the day is broken already.

Or let's say that you place an ad in the local paper and get a bill for the cost of the ad. Is that money you've spent today? Yes, it is. But will it show up in today's cheque stubs? No because you haven't paid it yet. Another hole in your simple model.

In fact, labelling a transaction a 'sale' or an 'expense' just isn't *specific* enough to allow most businesses to properly track what's going on. In practice, you'll need to use *two* labels for each transaction, something like: 'sale/cash' or 'sale/pay tomorrow', or 'expense/cheque today' or 'expense/just got the bill'. Generally two labels for each transaction are going to be enough to give you the flexibility to work out how your business is going.

Modern bookkeeping uses *two* labels for each transaction, which is why it's called **double entry**.

Example (This actually happened)

An engineer forms a consulting company and decides to build his own computer system to track how the company is going. In the system he has one list for *sales* (things he has done for clients that they will pay for) and another list for *expenses* (things the company has to pay for).

What could possibly go wrong?

The first thing that went wrong was that the system couldn't differentiate between general expenses (electricity, coffee) and travel expenses that needed to be invoiced to the customer (taxis, airfares). Then of course there was no way of differentiating between bills that were paid right away (phone bills for example) and bills that could wait (stationery). It wasn't long before the number of exceptions and extra lists and flags in the lists made the whole system unmaintainable and unusable.

The engineer in this story was me, and I wrote my own accounting system (in dBase III) that worked they way I described. And had the problems I described. Then I did an MBA and found out about double-entry accounting, threw away my homebrew system and bought a real one.

Moral: Don't try to reinvent something just because you can. And stick with double-entry bookkeeping because it works.

Accounts

We know that our model of a business has three things in it: assets, liability equity. We'll show them from now on in a list like this:

- assets
- liability
- equity

In practice you'll want to have a bit more detail than that. For example, money in the bank and cash in your till are both assets of the business, but it's useful to know how much of each you have. So you break the 'asset' label down into a number of more detailed labels (or *accounts*) like this:

- assets
-   bank
-   cash in hand
- liabilities
- equity

You traditionally show accounts in this way, with the highest-level ones sticking out to the left. In this case, if you know the total bank balance and the total cash in the till (usually called *cash in hand*) then you can add the two of them to find the company's total assets - which is the account at the level above them.

This is the general rule - if you have an account with indented accounts below it, like this:

- `account A`
- `account B`
- `account C`

... then the top one (account A) is going to be the total of the two lower ones (accounts B and C).

In practice, you're going to have other assets as well, so you simply add them to the list like this:

- `assets`
- `bank`
- `cash in hand`
- `stock`
- `debtors`
- `liabilities`
- `equity`

Things that you have in your shop for sale (**stock**) are assets, even though they're not money (yet!). And money owed to your company by customers is counted as **debtors**.

(Stock is sometimes also called **inventory**).

So in this **set of accounts** assets are the total of your bank balance, cash in hand, stock and debtors: money in the bank plus money in the till plus stock on the shelves plus money owed to the company.

Let's look at a couple of example **transactions** and see which pairs of labels you might put on them to categorise them.

A *cash sale* would labelled with 'cash in hand' (because the amount of cash in the till will change) and 'stock' (because you've sold something, so the amount of stock you have is less). We'll show transactions like this, without bullets:

```
Cash sale ... labels are:
   cash in hand
   stock
```

A *sale with payment tomorrow* would be 'stock' (because you've sold something) and 'debtors' (because the customer now owes you money).

```
Sale with payment tomorrow ...
labels are:
   debtors
   stock
```

When they come in and *pay what they owe*, that would be labelled as 'cash in hand' and 'debtors', because both of these are affected.

```
Payment for sale made yesterday ...
labels are:
   cash in hand
   debtors
```

Question

What accounts would be affected if you bought stock with cash?

Answer

Cash in hand and *stock*.

Explanation

The amount of cash in the till will change (because you've taken money out) and this is shown in your accounts as *cash in hand*. And the amount of *stock* will change (because you've just bought some new stuff).

Account balances, debits and credits

In an accounting system (either on a computer, or just on paper) you will have a list of these accounts with a **balance** against each one. For assets, the balance is just the value of that asset. So for example the balance for 'cash in hand' is the amount of cash in the till. The balance for 'debtors' is the total amount that people owe the company, and so on.

We'll show the balance on each account by just writing it next to the account name on the list:

- assets (total $55)
- bank $10
- cash in hand $15
- stock $20
- debtors $10
- liabilities $30
- equity $25

Notice that the assets account has a total which is the sum of all of the lower-level accounts under it: $55 = $10 + $15 + $20 + $10. Notice also that the accounting equation still holds (assets $55 = liabilities $30 + equity $25).

We've seen that each transaction has two 'labels', two accounts that it affects. In fact, you can think of a transaction as having two 'ends', each of which affects one account. One end is a **credit** (bad news) and the other end is a **debit** (good news).

So a cash sale has a credit ('bad news') effect on stock because your stock is now less but it has a debit ('good news') effect on cash in hand because you get some cash.

You will recognise the terms *credit* and *debit* from your bank statements and bills, but you might be confused because a 'debit' on your bank statement is generally a *bad* thing (it means you have less money in the bank). The reason is that the statement shows a 'debit' when something good happens *for the bank* (ie they owe you less money). But what's good for the bank is bad for you, so you've learned that 'debit' means bad news, even though it actually means 'good news'!

Every transaction has both a debit and a credit, and they both the debit and credit have the same value.

Here's an example of a transaction:

```
Cash sale
  credit: stock $10
  debit: cash in hand $10
```

The first line just tells us what the transaction is. The second line says that it affects the *stock* account. The second line says it also affects *cash in hand*. You'll notice that the same amount ($10) will be applied to each account.

The stock account will be **credited** (a bad thing: we have less stock) and the cash in hand account will be **debited** (a good thing: we have more money).

Question

What will the transaction look like where you make a
$10 sale to be paid for later?

Answer

```
Sale with payment later
   credit: stock $10
   debit: debtors $10
```

Explanation

Stock will be credited (a bad thing: we have less
stock) and debtors will be debited (a good thing:
someone owes us more money).

Account numbers and balances

In most computerised accounting
systems, each account has a name,
but it also has a number, like this:

- `1-1000 assets $10`

The number ("1-1000") is just so
that you can easily identify the account when you're
putting entries into the computer. There's nothing
special about the form of an *account number* (also
called an *account code*), except that some systems
will force you to use particular formats.

Note that the actual *amount* in an account ($10 in
this example) is always called the *balance*.

Balance sheet

If you list all of the accounts and their *balances*, this is called a *balance sheet*. It might look like this:

- assets (total $135)
-   bank $100
-   cash in hand $10
-   stock $20
-   debtors $5
- liabilities $15
- equity $120

Just as a check: assets ($135) = liabilities ($15) + equity ($120).

When accountants are trained, they are told that there are two more pieces of information that they *must* put on every balance sheet: the company name and the date. That's just good practice, so that if you have a number of balance sheets floating around (for different companies, or for the same company for different dates) you don't get confused.

So here's our complete balance sheet:

```
Sample Company Limited
Balance sheet at 1Jan2020
```
- assets (total $135)
-   bank $100
-   cash in hand $10
-   stock $20
-   debtors $5
- liabilities $15
- equity $120

Now let's say that we make a sale on 2Jan2020; we sell $10 of stock and get $10 more cash in hand. The **transaction record** for that sale would look like this:

```
Sale on 2Jan2020
  credit: stock $10
  debit: cash in hand $10
```

Remember 'credit' means 'bad news', 'debit' means 'good news', and they have to be the same dollar value.

The new balance sheet will look like this:

```
Sample Company Limited
Balance sheet at 2Jan2020
 •   assets (total $135)
 •     bank $100
 •     cash in hand $20
 •     stock $10
 •     debtors $5
 •   liabilities $15
 •   equity $120
```

So the value of 'stock' has gone down by $10 (a bad thing - a credit) but the value of 'cash in hand' has gone up by $10 (a good thing - a debit).

Notice that the balance sheet at 1Jan is different to the balance sheet at 2Jan. It's good to think of a balance sheet as a 'snapshot' of the balances of all of its accounts at the particular date on the top of it.

Question

If we make a sale for $5 on 3Jan to be paid later, what would the balance sheet for 4Jan look like?

Answer

```
Sample Company Limited
Balance sheet at 4Jan2020
```
- assets (total $135)
-   bank $100
-   cash in hand $20
-   stock $5
-   debtors $10
- liabilities $15
- equity $120

Explanation

The transaction record would look like this:

```
Sale for payment later on 3Jan2020
  credit: stock $5
  debit: debtors $5
```

Stock would be credited (a bad thing: we have less stock) and debtors would be debited (a good thing: someone owes us $5).

So you'll see in the new balance sheet that stock has changed from $10 to $5 and debtors has changed from $5 to $10.

Ledgers

In the days before computers (and accounting has been around since at least the 16th century) people used to write their transactions in a book called a **ledger**.

So there would be a book in the shop with handwritten entries like this one:

```
Cash sale on 1Jan1517
  credit: stock $10
  debit: cash in hand $10
```

At the end of each month, the shopowner would construct a new version of the balance sheet to see how the business was doing. They would do that by getting another book with one page for each account, and by **posting** each transaction into the account book by writing each transaction against the two accounts that it was debiting/crediting. Then they would summarise the totals for each account in a balance sheet.

Of course these days we have computers to do all of this posting and totalling for us. Most accounting software will let you just put in the transactions and it will do all of the hard work of calculating the balance sheet at the press of a button.

Aside

You can imagine that a paper ledger would get a bit tatty after a while. In fact, when businesses wanted to falsify their records to cheat on tax, they'd have to create a brand new *set of books* and then put them in an oven to make them look old and tatty: *cooking the books*. No, I'm not joking.

Business value

So does the balance sheet tell you
the value of a business? Sadly, no.
The equity value on the balance
sheet tells you how much the
company 'owes' its owners. It's
what would be left if the company collected all of its
debts and sold everything. Technically it's called the
book value of the company.

But business are more than just their book value;
there's also the future income that the company will
generate. So if you try to buy a business you'll pay the
book value *plus* a negotiated amount (which in
accounting terms is called **goodwill**).

The way people negotiate the amount of goodwill is
by talking about **multiples**. Basically you look at the
amount of profit that the company made in each of
the past few years, and multiply it by some value.
Typical business *multiples* are between 3 and 20
depending on what the business is likely to do in
future (and also how motivated the buyer and seller
are!).

Current and non-current, ratios

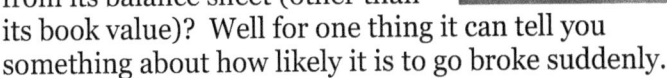

What can you tell about a business from its balance sheet (other than its book value)? Well for one thing it can tell you something about how likely it is to go broke suddenly.

First, let's look at those 'liabilities' in the balance sheet. Remember: a liability is something the company owes to someone (other than the owners). There are many different things that might end up under liabilities: tax owed to the government, bills to be paid, long-term loans from the bank.

Liabilities are usually broken down in the balance sheet into ***current liabilities*** and ***non-current liabilities*** like this:

- liabilities (total $1095)
- current liabilities (total $95)
- tax payable ($35)
- trade creditors ($60)
- non-current liabilities (total $1000)
- bank loan $1000

Current liabilities are things that have to be paid soon (say within a year).

So if you have a balance sheet that looks like this:

```
Sample Company Limited
Balance sheet at 2Jan2020
```
- assets (total $5500)
- bank $300
- cash in hand $100
- stock $1000
- debtors $100
- building fitout $4000
- liabilities (total $4000)
- current liabilities $3000
- non-current liabilities $1000
- equity $1500

... you can see that you have a company that will have to find $3000 sometime in the coming year, but that only has $300 in the bank and $100 in cash today. Of course, there are no hard and fast rules, but this doesn't look good.

In the same way as you can split liabilities into current and non-current, you can also do the same for assets: **current assets** and **non-current assets**.

Current assets are assets that the business can turn into cash within a year. So the bank balance is a current asset, as is the money in the till. But the building fitout? Probably not. Let's assume that building fitout isn't considered a current asset; the balance sheet will look like this:

```
Sample Company Limited
Balance sheet at 2Jan2020
• assets (total $5500)
•    current assets (total $1500)
•       bank $300
•       cash in hand $100
•       debtors $100
•       stock $1000
•    non-current assets (total $4000)
•       building fitout $4000
• liabilities (total $4000)
•    current liabilities $3000
•    non-current liabilities $1000
• equity $1500
```

One way of measuring just how bad things are is to calculate the **current ratio**, which is current assets / current liabilities. For the above company this is $1500/$4000 = 0.375 There are many rules of thumb around this ratio, but in general low is bad, high is good.

Another ratio people use is the **quick ratio**, which is (current assets - stock) / current liabilities which for the above company is ($1500-$1000)/$4000 = 0.125 Again, the higher the better.

More on transactions

I said earlier that there are two parts to each transaction, a credit ('bad news') part and a debit ('good news') part. Actually there can be more than one credit and more than one debit, as long as the credit and debit amounts match (they **balance**).

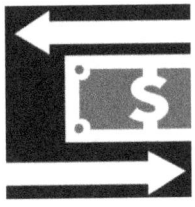

For example, let's say that a customer buys $10 worth of stock, and pays $5 now but will pay the rest later.

Remember that earlier we showed a cash sale like this:

```
Sale on 2Jan2020
  credit: stock $10
  debit: cash in hand $10
```

If this had been a sale for credit it would have looked like this:

```
Sale on 2Jan2020
  credit: stock $10
  debit: debtors $10
```

So how do we show this part-cash, part-debtor transaction? Like this:

```
Sale on 2Jan2020
  credit: stock $10
  debit: cash in hand $5
  debit: debtors $5
```

As long as the total amount of credit(s) equals the total amount of debit(s) then it will still work.

Retained income

Of course, there's only one reason to run a business: to make money.

What happens when you sell some stock that cost you $2, and get $3 in cash for it? Stock will be credited by $2 (stock is less, that's bad news, which is a credit) and cash in hand will be debited (good news) by $3. The value of the company (equity) will increase by $1 (bad news for the company, because it owes its owners more, so another credit), like this:

```
Cash sale
   credit: stock $2
   debit: cash in hand $3
   credit: equity $1
```

Check that this is balanced (total debits = total credits).

In practice, equity is split into two parts: ***paid-in capital*** and ***retained earnings***, just so you can see what's going on. Paid-in capital is the amount of money that the owners first put into the company when it was formed. All other changes to equity due to profits or losses are shown as retained earnings.

So let's look at the complete lifecycle of a company from its formation.

```
Sample Company Limited
Balance sheet at 1Jan2020
• assets (total $10)
•     stock $0
•     cash in hand $10
• liabilities $0
• equity (total $10)
•     paid-in capital $10
•     retained earnings $0
```

The company has just been formed, and the owner has put in $10 in cash.

Now the company buys some stock:

```
Purchase of stock on 2Jan2020
  credit: cash in hand $2
  debit: stock $2
```

Note that the value of the stock in the balance sheet is the price you *paid* for it, not the price you hope to *sell* it for.

The balance sheet now looks like this:

```
Sample Company Limited
Balance sheet at 2Jan2020
• assets (total $10)
•     stock $2
•     cash in hand $8
• liabilities $0
• equity (total $10)
•     paid-in capital $10
•     retained earnings $0
```

Now you sell the stock for $3 (yippee!):

```
Sale of stock on 3Jan2020
  debit: cash in hand $3
  credit: stock $2
  credit: retained earnings $1
```

The balance sheet now looks like this:

```
Sample Company Limited
Balance sheet at 3Jan2020
• assets (total $11)
•   stock $0
•   cash in hand $11
• liabilities $0
• equity (total $11)
•   paid-in capital $10
•   retained earnings $1
```

You can still see the amount that was put in to start the company ($10 paid-in capital) and you can also see the profit to date ($1 retained earnings).

Bank reconciliation

Every business will have one or more bank accounts, and these are just treated as assets. The only difference is that both you and the bank will have an opinion about the balance of that account, and you need to make sure that those opinions agree, or at least figure out why they disagree.

Why bother? Well, it's only through this process that you can find out if your bank is honest. Also, it will allow you to figure out which cheques you've written that have got lost in the mail, and which payments you think you've received but that haven't made it into your bank account. It also allows you to record the various charges that your bank makes.

You will do this by a process called **reconciliation**. It starts with you getting a bank statement, either electronically or on paper. If your bank doesn't automatically send you statements each month, you'll have to generate one yourself.

Your accounting system will let you tag which of the transactions that you've entered have appeared on a bank statement, so the reconciliation process means opening your accounting system and finding one by one the transactions that are on the bank statement, and checking them off. You will then enter the **closing balance** from your bank statement and if all is well, you can just file it: reconciliation is complete.

If there's a discrepancy (ie if the closing balance from the bank doesn't match what your accounting system thinks it should be) then you have a problem. Usually it's simple things like writing a different amount on a cheque (or an electronic payment) than you entered into your accounting system. But sometimes it's fraud, so it's worth checking.

Once your accounting system has done its reconciliation, you can also ask it to print a **reconciliation report**. This shows transactions that you have put into your accounting system, but which for some reason haven't shown up yet in your bank statements. Any old transactions on this report might indicate payments or receipts that have got lost and need to be chased up.

Resist at all costs the temptation to brush discrepancies 'under the carpet'! If your bank reconciliation is out by $0.01 you might be tempted to just enter a different closing balance just to make the problem go away. Don't. There's a general rule in reconciliations: if there's a $0.01 discrepancy, it will generally be because there are two errors: one for $100,000 in one direction and the other for $100,000.01 in the other direction.

Profit and loss

Of course, one of the things you'd like to do is to find out how your business is doing this week, or this month, or this year. Accounting systems provide a set of *profit and loss accounts* to answer these questions.

Technically these accounts are actually part of the retained earnings account, so the whole set of accounts for a company will look like this:

- assets
- liabilities
- equity
- paid-in capital
- retained earnings
- income
- expenses

So when the company gets income, say from the sale of $2 worth of stock for $3, the transaction looks like this:

```
Sale of stock
   credit: stock $2
   debit: cash in hand $3
   credit: income $1
```

This credit of the 'income' account will also increase retained earnings and total equity. (Although this is a profit, it's a bad thing for the company because it now owes its owners $1 more, so it's 'bad news': a credit.)

In practice, these profit and loss accounts are displayed in a completely separate way in your accounting system, as if they weren't part of the balance sheet at all.

The profit and loss accounts actually form their own set, which has its own mini accounting equation: profit = income - expenses.

```
Sample Company Limited
Profit and Loss accounts for 1-31
January 2020
• income $1
• expenses $0
• profit $1
```

Something else that's different about profit and loss accounts is that when you see them in a report (like the *P&L report* shown above) they are reported for a period (1-31 January 2020) rather than at a particular date (like a balance sheet).

Using profit and loss accounts

Let's look at what happens in your accounting system which you use one of these P&L accounts. Here's the sale transaction:

```
Sale of stock
  credit: stock $2
  debit: cash in hand $3
  credit: income $1
```

The 'stock' and 'cash in hand' accounts are in the balance sheet, so they will change. The 'income' account is in the P&L so it will change too ... but as 'income' is really part of 'retained earnings', then 'retained earnings' and 'equity' will change as well. Here's the full set of accounts before the transaction:

```
Sample Company Limited
Balance sheet at 1Jan2020
• assets (total $10)
•    cash in hand $0
•    stock $10
• liabilities $0
• equity (total $10)
•    paid-in capital $10
•    retained earnings $0

Profit and loss for Jan2020
• income $0
• expenses $0
• profit $0
```

Now here's that transaction again:

```
Sale of stock
  credit: stock $2
  debit: cash in hand $3
  credit: income $1
```

And here's how the accounts would look the following day:

```
Sample Company Limited
Balance sheet at 2Jan2020
• assets (total $11)
•    cash in hand $3
•    stock $8
• liabilities $0
• equity (total $11)
•    paid-in capital $10
•    retained earnings $1

Profit and loss for Jan2020
• income $1
• expenses $0
• profit $1
```

So the two balance sheet accounts 'stock' and 'cash in hand' have been changed directly, and the change to the 'income' account has automatically increased 'profit' (which is just calculated from income-expenses) and also 'retained earnings' (which is just calculated from profit) and also equity (which is calculated from retained earnings).

If you're having trouble following this, try thinking of the accounts this way:

- `assets`
- `liabilities`
- `equity`
-   `paid-in capital`
-   `retained earnings`
-     `profit`
-       `income`
-       `expenses`

You can see that a change in income will cause a change in profit, retained earnings and equity because they're just totals. Your accounting system shows them in a different order (and in fact in two completely separate sets) but this is what's really going on under the hood.

Debits, credits and expenses

Okay, here's the only bit of accounting that completely did my head in when I studied it. When the company spends money it shows up as an *increase* in expenses, which *reduces* profit and therefore *reduces* retained earnings and *reduces* equity, which is ... a good thing (a debit)  because the company owes the owners less. So an increase in expenses is ... a good thing (ie a debit) - ???!!.

Now that's *completely* counter-intuitive. Increasing expenses means less profit, which must be a *bad* thing, surely? No, it's a *good* thing because from the company's point of view it ends up owing you less.

At this point you start to see why accounting is usually taught pretty much by rote, rather than by reason. No other accounting text I've seen will tell you that debit = good and credit = bad, they just say "here are the rules for whether a debit or credit will increase or decrease a given account - just learn them".

If it helps, here are the rules:

```
assets, expenses: debit = +, credit
= -
liabilities, equity, income: debit =
-, credit = +
```

Personally, I prefer to remember that it all makes sense except expenses!

Question

What would the transaction record look like when a company received a bill for $10 for electricity?

Answer

```
Electricity bill
  credit: liabilities $10
  debit: expenses $10
```

Explanation

The two accounts that would be affected are liabilities (because we owe the electricity company $10) and expenses (which would eventually affect retained earnings and finally equity).

The effect on liabilities would be a credit (a bad thing: liabilities would be increased).

The effect on expenses would be a debit (expenses would be increased).

Dividends

When the company has made enough money the owners will generally want to get some of it out and spend it. There are a couple of ways they can do this: if it's a small business and the

owners actually work in the business, they can pay themselves a salary.

The other way is to **declare a dividend**. This is a special payment made to the owners by the company that reduces the equity of the company (if the equity is a loan from the owners to the company, then a **dividend** is a repayment of part of that loan).

Dividend payment shows up in the balance sheet under equity:

- equity
- paid-in capital
- retained earnings
- dividends paid

And the transaction of actually paying a dividend looks like this:

```
Dividend payment
  credit: bank $10
  debit: dividends paid $10
```

(Reducing the bank account by $10 is bad news, so a credit. Reducing equity by $10 is good news (for the company) so it's a debit).

Negative balances, depreciation and bad debts

Debits and credits change accounts balances in different directions depending on which account is involved. So for example, a debit (good news) applied to an asset account like your bank account will *increase*

it (because if your assets increase that's a good thing), but a debit (good news) applied to a liability account like a bank debt will *decrease* it (because if your debts decrease that's a good thing too).

Of course, if you decrease the balance in an account enough it will go negative. No problem with that. In fact some accounts are actually intended to be negative.

Here's an example: if you buy a computer for $1000 it will show up as an asset in your accounts:

- `assets`
- `  equipment at cost $1000`

But we all know that a computer you bought yesterday for $1000 can't be sold for $1000 tomorrow. In fact, the tax department will let you reduce the value of some of your assets over time in a process called **depreciation**. (This reflects the fact that the value of most assets *does* decrease '**depreciate**' over time.)

Why does the tax department care about the value of your assets? Because your company pays tax on the profit it makes each year, and depreciation allows you to make the profit look smaller and so reduce the amount of tax you pay ... and the government *does* care about that!

So here's what a depreciation account looks like. Beside the account that shows the value of the asset 'equipment' there's a negative account that shows the amount that that asset has depreciated:

- ` assets  (total $800)`
- `    equipment at cost $1000`
- `    depreciation on equipment -$200`

There are complex rules that set out exactly how much you can depreciate each type of asset each year. In practice, most businesses leave all this to their accountants, and the depreciation amounts are added to your books at the end of each financial year.

The transaction that creates the depreciation will look like this:

```
Depreciation on computer at
31Dec2020
  debit: expenses $200
  credit: depreciation on equipment
$200
```

As a result of this transaction expenses will go up (a good thing, remember, because it reduces equity) and depreciation will go down (a bad thing because it will reduce assets).

Notice that the value of the assets is now $800, but we haven't lost sight of what we originally paid for the computer.

A fancy name for the depreciation account is a **contra-asset**. Another example of a contra-asset account is 'allowance for bad and doubtful debts' which is an account that comes next to the debtors account.

The 'bad and doubtful debts' account you put through a transaction like this:

```
Allowance for bad debt
  debit: expenses $100
  credit: bad and doubtful debt $100
```

This will increase expenses by $100 and reduce bad and doubtful debts to make it negative.

In the balance sheet you'll see something like this:

- `assets (total $1000)`
- `debtors $1100`
- `bad and doubtful debts -$100`

Working with an accountant

Using an accountant is not compulsory: there's no law that says you have to use one to do your accounts at the end of each year (unless you are required by law to use a special sort of accountant called an **auditor** to check that your accounts are complete and correct).

So for most businesses an accountant is not compulsory. Unfortunately in most countries the tax laws that govern things like depreciation are so complex that if you don't use and accountant *you'll wish that you had*.

Accountants come in a variety of characters, and you'll need to choose one that suits you. Some accountants are very conservative, and will insist that you pay exactly the amount of tax that you should - in some cases, perhaps slightly more than you should, just to be on the safe side.

Other accounts like you to take risks, and will bend your accounts slightly so that you pay the absolute minimum in tax. Notice that I said "you ... take risks", because at the end of the day it's you and your business that's taking all of the risks: no accountant ever had to pay the tax and fines that their client was hit with when the government caught up with them. Although to be fair some have gone to jail for helping their clients take absolute liberties with the tax system.

So if a fried of yours says his accountant has "saved him a lot of money" what that really means is that his accountant has "put him at a lot of risk". Just bear that in mind when you're choosing an accountant.

Most accountants will charge you by the hour, but if you're canny you'll negotiate a fixed price for your business after the first year or so of using that accountant. Being charged by the hour can mean that every time you call them with a query it goes on your bill.

If you use a piece of accounting software then you will probably want the accountant to set up your **chart of accounts**. This is just the list of balance sheet and P&L accounts that your system will be set up with.

The level of interaction between you and your accountant will depend mainly on the size of your business. If you run a tiny business then you may use the 'shoebox' method - this is where you just dump all of your bills and invoices into a shoebox and hand it to your accountant at the end of each month.

If your business is a bit bigger you will probably want to employ a **bookkeeper**. This is someone who does the basic data entry into your accounting system: you might only need a bookkeeper part-time, depending on how many transactions you do a week.

If you have a bookkeeper then you'll generally give your accountant a copy of your accounting system files just after the end of the financial year. They will then analyse them and give you back a set of **year-end transactions** which include things like depreciation, tax liabilities and other stuff to tidy up your accounts. You will then put these transactions into your accounting system. Your accountant will also fill in your tax return and give it to you to sign.

Rollovers

For some reason, some accounting systems force you to delete all of last year's data at some point during the year. This means making a copy of your accounting system files before the data is deleted, so that you can refer to it later.

The process of deleting the old data is called *rollover*, and it's generally done in two phases: *payroll rollover* and *financial year rollover*. Payroll rollover deletes the payroll information, and the other rollover deletes the rest.

You'll generally have to wait until your accountant has given you the year-end transaction, and you've input them, before you do the financial year rollover.

Accruals

There are actually two different ways you can run your accounts: **cash method** and **accrual method**. In practice no-one in their right mind will run the cash method. Let me explain why.

In the cash method, you only enter bills into your accounting system when you *pay* them. In the accrual method, you enter them as soon as you *receive* them.

The same goes for income: in the cash method you only count income when you are paid it. In the accrual method you count it when you invoice it.

So the difference between cash and accrual is that with the cash method you have no idea what's about to happen: you have no visibility of bills that you have to pay, and no visibility of cash that's going to come in.

Needless to say, most businesses run on an accrual basis.

You can also do some fairly nifty things using accruals. Let's say that you pay rent at the end of each quarter. You might find that your profit for each month of the quarter is positive, but you always make a loss in the last month because that's when the rent expense shows up. Although this is accurate, it doesn't give you a very good picture of how your business is doing; it looks like it's a dog one month every quarter.

So what you can do is to **accrue** the rent expense as a balance sheet item when the rent bill comes in:

```
Rent accrual for June quarter
   credit: bank account $3000
   debit: rent accrual $3000
```

This means that you now have a balance sheet account with $1000 sitting in it:

- `liabilities`
- `rent accrual $3000`

... and then you set up four separate transactions, one a week, to **expense** the rent and allocate it to each week:

```
Monthly rent expense
   credit: rent accrual $1000
   debit: rent expense $1000
```

So now you've got a record of when you paid the rent bill, but you haven't stuffed up your profit calculation for each week.

Of course, not all months have the same number of days in them. You could get really technical and expense the rent at slightly more for long months and slightly less for short months - but although that might be fun to do (well, for some of us!) it's probably not worth the effort. In any event, it's important that the rent accrual account ends up at zero at the end of the financial year.

Note that it's only worth doing this sort of thing if it's stuffing up your knowledge of how your business in travelling week to week or month to month. There's no point in doing accruals for minor expenses ... unless you want to do it just for fun, in which case

you've got bigger problems than measuring
profitability.

Cashflow

One disadvantage of the accrual method is that it leaves you blind to problems with **cashflow**.

It can happen like this: you set up your company and put in $10 as paid-in capital, then you buy some stock for $5 and pay cash for it. Now your balance sheet looks like this:

- assets (total $10)
-   bank $5
-   stock $5
-   debtors $0
- liabilities $0
- equity (total $10)
-   paid-in capital $10
-   retained earnings $0

Now you sell that stock to a company down the road for $20 (which they say they will pay later), so your company looks like this:

- assets (total $25)
-   bank $5
-   stock $0
-   debtors $20
- liabilities $0
- equity (total $25)
-   paid-in capital $10
-   retained earnings $15

We've made a profit of $15! So we rush out and buy $15 worth of stock. We've only got $5 in the bank so we ask the supplier to send us a bill for $15, which we will have to pay in 30 days.

The bill from the stock supplier ends up in a liability account called **accounts payable**:

- assets (total $40)
- bank $5
- stock $15
- debtors $20
- liabilities (total $15)
- accounts payable $15
- equity (total $25)
- paid-in capital $10
- retained earnings $15

This still looks pretty healthy. We have cash in the bank, we have stock and we have made a profit of $15 all up. What could possibly go wrong?

Here's the problem: we have to pay our stock supplier $15 in 30 days, but unless our customer pays the $20 they owe us before then, *we won't have enough cash to pay the supplier.*

If our customer decides to pay us after 60, or even 90 days (despite what it says on our invoice, despite their assurances that they pay promptly, despite your contract with them) then we're going to run out of cash.

This is called a **cashflow crisis** and it kills more new businesses than anything else.

What happens in practice is that you get into a death spiral where: you can't pay your staff, so they leave; you can't pay your suppliers so they stop supplying you; you spend all of your time on the phone chasing people who owe you money, and avoiding people who are trying to get money from you; and you can't pay your taxes so you end up in jail.

And all this while running a profitable company!

So how do you avoid cashflow problems? There are a number of ways of doing it. The best way is to be **conservative**.

When you made your decision to buy more stock, instead of buying $15 worth of stock you could have bought $5 worth (the amount we have in the bank). Then regardless of how long your customer took to pay, you could always just pay cash when the bill was due.

The disadvantage: your business will grow more slowly.

Another approach is to use **cashflow modelling**, which means putting into your accounting system your best guess on when various bills are due, and when you're likely to be paid by your customers.

The disadvantage: if customers don't pay when you expect them to, you've got a problem.

Another approach is to get a **line of credit**. This is an arrangement with a bank to lend you money when you need it. So if your customer pays late, you can just borrow the money you need - you'll have to pay interest on it, but that's better than going broke.

Most banks will ask for **security** for any sort of loan. Usually this means your house.

One way of thinking about cashflow is to think in terms of **funding**.

If you buy $5 worth of stock and sell it you have to 'fund' the $5. The more stock you buy the more you have to fund. Funding can come from the bank, or from the company's cash, or from additional investment by you or your partners.

This is particularly valid in cases where you make a sale before you have to buy the stock. In this case, each sale has its own *funding requirement*. Depending on how much money you have to spare, you might even put some controls on what your staff are allowed to sell, so that the funding doesn't cause you to have cashflow problems later.

Another useful concept is the idea of **working capital**. This is the amount of money that you leave in your company's bank account to allow for the fact that not everyone pays on time, and that sometimes bills come in that you weren't expecting. Personally, I'm quite comfortable with a large amount of cash just sitting in a bank account gaining no interest because it helps me sleep. But I'm ultra-conservative (about money).

Question

You run a recruitment company that hires out accountants. A customer calls up and wants to hire an accountant for three months at $12,000 a month. You pay your contract accountant $5000 a month.

Your accountant gets paid at the end of each month, and you send an invoice to your customer when you pay the accountant. But your customer takes two months to pay.

How much funding will you need to cover this sale?

Answer

$15,000

Explanation

At the end of month 1 you'll have to pay out $5000 to the accountant. The same at the end of month 2, and month 3: total paid up to that point will be $15,000.

If you're lucky, your customer will pay you $12,000 for the first invoice - but will pay two months after your first invoice: ie your first payment will arrive at the end of month 3. Let's be conservative and say the payment will arrive a week or two late.

At the end of month 3 you will have paid out $15,000 and got no cash from your customer. So when you make the sale you'd better have $15,000 free, otherwise you're going to be in trouble.

By way of contract, your cash flow and profit for each month will look like this:

```
          Total        Total
          Cash flow    Profit
 Month 1   -$5,000      $7,000
 Month 2  -$10,000     $14,000
 Month 3  -$15,000     $21,000
 Month 4   -$3,000     $21,000
 Month 5    $9,000     $21,000
 Month 6   $21,000     $21,000
```

You'll notice that the profit of $21,000 turns up in the cash flow finally at Month 6 (when the final bill is paid by the customer). But that it drops right down to -$15,000 at Month 3.

Accounts receivable

The part of your business that collects money from customers (ie debtors) is called **accounts receivable**. The process of collecting money in a retail business is pretty straightforward: you either take cash from the customer at the point of sale, or you take a credit card.

With business customers (this is sometimes called **B2B** for business-to-business sales) the process is a lot more complicated.

It goes like this: first you have to get some sort of paperwork to prove that you've actually made the sale (the reason for this will become clear later). This might be a signature on a delivery docket, or a purchase order from your customer.

Then after you deliver the goods or services, you send an **invoice**.

An invoice is not a legal document - it's just a reminder that they have to pay. Generally your **payment terms** (how long they have before they have to pay) are shown on the invoice. So you mail the invoice and wait.

Often at the end of each month you will send **statements** to all of your customers. These are reports from your accounting system that show which invoices are still not paid yet (these are said to be **outstanding**, not in the sense that they're really really good, but in the sense that they stand out as not having been paid yet!).

Eventually your customer may pay, and they will generally put money straight into your bank account and send a **remittance advice** to tell you which invoice they've just paid.

Your accounting system can at any time give you a
picture of who owes what for how long: this is called
an *aged receivables* report, and it looks like this:

Customer	Total	0-30	31-60	61-90	90+
ABC co	$100		$100		
DEF co	$200		$120		$80
XYZ co	$150	$150			
	$450	$150	$220		$80

This shows all of the customers that owe you money
(I've just called them ABC co, DEF co for simplicity:
the real report would show actual customer names).

The total that each company owes you is shown
under the heading "Total".

Each amount they owe is also split across the page
according to how long it's been since we generated
the invoice. The numbers across the top (0-30, etc)
are numbers of days. So for ABC co, they owe us
$100, which is for one or more invoices we sent them
between 31 and 60 days ago.

Obviously the stuff to the right of the page is the stuff
you worry about. DEF co have owed us $80 for more
than 90 days. This could be due to a number of
things: a) the invoice got lost in the post (which is
why we send statements) b) they are having their own
cashflow crisis or c) they forgot.

Generally by the time an invoice reaches 31-60 you
should be calling the customer and asking them when
they're going to pay.

By the time it gets past 90 days you should be
threatening them with legal action.

A good way to deal with accounts receivable is to have
someone (could be you, as the business owner) call
all of the companies that have owed you money for,

say, 30 or more days and ask them when they're going to pay.

If you make sure this happens once a week, and if the person who does it escalates to the owner any customer that seems to have a problem paying, then you can keep accounts receivable problems from getting too big.

If you do need to take legal action, you'll need to prove that you actually made the sale. Your invoice is not proof of that, but your original proof of sale (purchase order, signed delivery docket, etc) that we talked about earlier, is. Which is why you asked for it in the first place.

Setting payment terms

You might think that the best way to avoid cashflow problems is to simply set your payment terms to 7 days. That way, everyone will pay you quickly and you have no problem.

There are two setbacks to this approach: first, some of your customers will insist that they want longer to pay than your 7 days (they have cash flow to worry about as well). The second is that most clients will happily agree to pay you on 7 days, but will then actually take 45 days to pay. And as long as they pay eventually there's not much you can do about it.

So my attitude is: set short payment terms, but expect the worst.

Very large companies and governments often have an additional issue: because of the way their internal systems work they can't pay any sooner than 60 (or even 90 or 120) days even if they want to. If you get an order from one of these companies it's worth asking them how long they usually take to pay, just so you can bear that in mind while you're working out your cashflow.

Very small companies have yet another problem: they run out of cash and *can't* pay. Sometimes they can't pay on time, sometimes they just go broke and disappear. So if you sell to very small companies who might do this, get them to **pay in advance**.

In your accounting system you'll show this as a liability in an account called **customer prepayments**, which will be debited (credit goes straight to income) when you actually deliver the goods or services.

Accounts Payable

Your accounting system will generate a similar report for things that you have bought, but not yet paid for. It's called an **aged payables** report and it works the same as an aged receivables report.

Supplier	Total	0-30	31-60	61-90	90+
GHI co	$10		$10		
JKL co	$250		$170		$80
	$260		$180		$80

Of course the only way that your accounting system knows you owe money is if you tell it. You'll generally do this by entering a record of a **purchase** into your system.

This is trickier than it sounds because unlike invoices, cheques and other things you won't be generating a paper or electronic record of a purchase when you actually buy something. Let me give you an example.

Let's say that a rep comes into your business and offers to sell you some stock. You fill out an order form and sign it, and the rep will give you a copy of the form for your records.

Because you're busy you'll likely put the order form in a pile and forget about it. Then the goods will arrive, along with an invoice from the supplier.

So at that point you might put the invoice into your accounting system as a purchase, and it will show up on your aged payables report.

So now you owe the supplier money. But you're *actually* owed them money from the moment you signed the order form. If you don't enter the purchase until you get the invoice, you'll have an incorrect picture of how much money you owe.

Moral: enter the purchase when you make the purchase. Then you'll know how much you have to pay and when, and be able to manage it.

Limited company, insolvent trading

What would happen if a company's liabilities were *more* than its assets? Let's say that the company has $10 in the bank but gets a bill for $11 rent. Then assets ($10) = liabilities ($11) + equity, so the equity must be -$1.

This is called **negative equity** and it generally happens just before a business fails miserably.

Now, on the face of it if the owner of the company is 'owed' minus $1 by the company you might think that the owner has to put in another $1 to pay the company's debts. And this used to be true before the **limited liability** company was invented.

For a 'limited liability' company, the owners don't have to help meet the debts of the company ... they can just walk away. As a supplier doing business with that sort of company you have an added risk - you might not get paid. That's why there is a legal requirement for all limited liability companies to always show the 'limited' in their name: so that everyone doing business with them knows about the additional risk.

So what's to stop someone setting up a company, having it run up huge debts and then walking away?

Well as well as one or more owners, each company has to have one or more **directors**. These are people who take personal responsibility for the way the company is run. If you're a company director you have to make sure that if the company looks like it might get into negative equity, you stop the company from trading.

Another name for having negative equity is *insolvency*, and for a director, allowing a company to ***trade while insolvent*** is an offence that can (in theory) end up with you in jail.

Company directors may or may not be owners of the company. For large companies, directors are simply employees who get paid to look after the company. If something goes wrong the owners are still protected.

In a small company, the owners are usually the directors. So if you decide to run up big debts in your company and then walk away, you may end up in jail.

(By the way, some companies give senior people a job title that includes the word 'Director'. These people may or may not be actual directors of the company; there will be a government register that shows who the actual directors of each company are.)

Taxes and insurance

You'll notice that I haven't mentioned **taxes** at all so far. That's simply because they're different in different places and almost anything I might tell you  about taxes in New South Wales, Australia may or may not be true in another country (or even another Australian State!).

My suggestion is that you call your local government office responsible for small business and ask them what taxes you should be paying and how. They're usually fairly good at this, and after all you're paying for them to do it. Remember there are tax implications both for your employees (you will generally have to take tax out of their pay and send it to the government) and your business (your accountant should sort that out at the end of the financial year). There may also be separate Federal, State and local taxes, so ask around.

Of course most companies have some form of **insurance** against fire, theft, and so on. But there are also sometimes **statutory insurances** for things like worker's compensation which the law says that you have to have as well. The government should be able to tell you what these are.

Not doing the right thing about tax and statutory insurance can get you into jail, so it's worth finding out!

Even where insurance isn't required by law it's sometimes a good idea. The basic forms of insurance available for businesses usually fall into these classes: fire and theft, public liability, professional indemnity. I'll cover these one by one.

Fire and theft insurance is what it says: if someone breaks in or your place burns down, you get paid.

Public liability is insurance against the possibility that someone will come onto your premises (even if they break in!) and will hurt themselves and then sue you. It's pretty unlikely, so the insurance is fairly cheap.

Professional indemnity is generally only for companies that sell services. It's insurance against the possibility that one of your customers will be upset enough about the advice or work that you've done for them and will sue you. The cost of this will depend on what kind of business you have.

Note that many of your customers (particularly large ones) will insist that you have public liability and possibly also professional indemnity insurance before they'll buy anything from you, so it's a good idea to call a couple of potential large customers and ask them what they usually require.

You might also want to talk to an **insurance broker**. This is a kind of travel agent for insurance: they will shop around for you and give you advice.

Remember that if you pay for insurance in one lump you can accrue it over the period of insurance so it doesn't make one month look like a stinker. (You should know what this means by now - otherwise re-read the section on Accruals).

What's next?

If you've enjoyed reading this book as much as I've enjoyed writing it, please go here:

```
www.amazon.com/dp/B00ESUOEW8
```

to submit a review to encourage others to read it.

If you hated the book and want to warn others not to buy it, use the same link and write a bad review!

If you'd like to see what other books I've written, you can do that here:

```
www.amazon.com/-/e/B001KD4070
```

Much of what I've written has been fiction (but not this book, honest!).

If you're about to start your own company, congratulations. I've been running companies for many decades and I can tell you that it's the most fun you can have sitting down.

Index